Chanukah

Dear Devon,

I hope you enjoy this book

Always remember that

"things are not always what they seem"

I love you,

Daddy

RE-ZOOM

ISTVAN BANYAI

VIKING

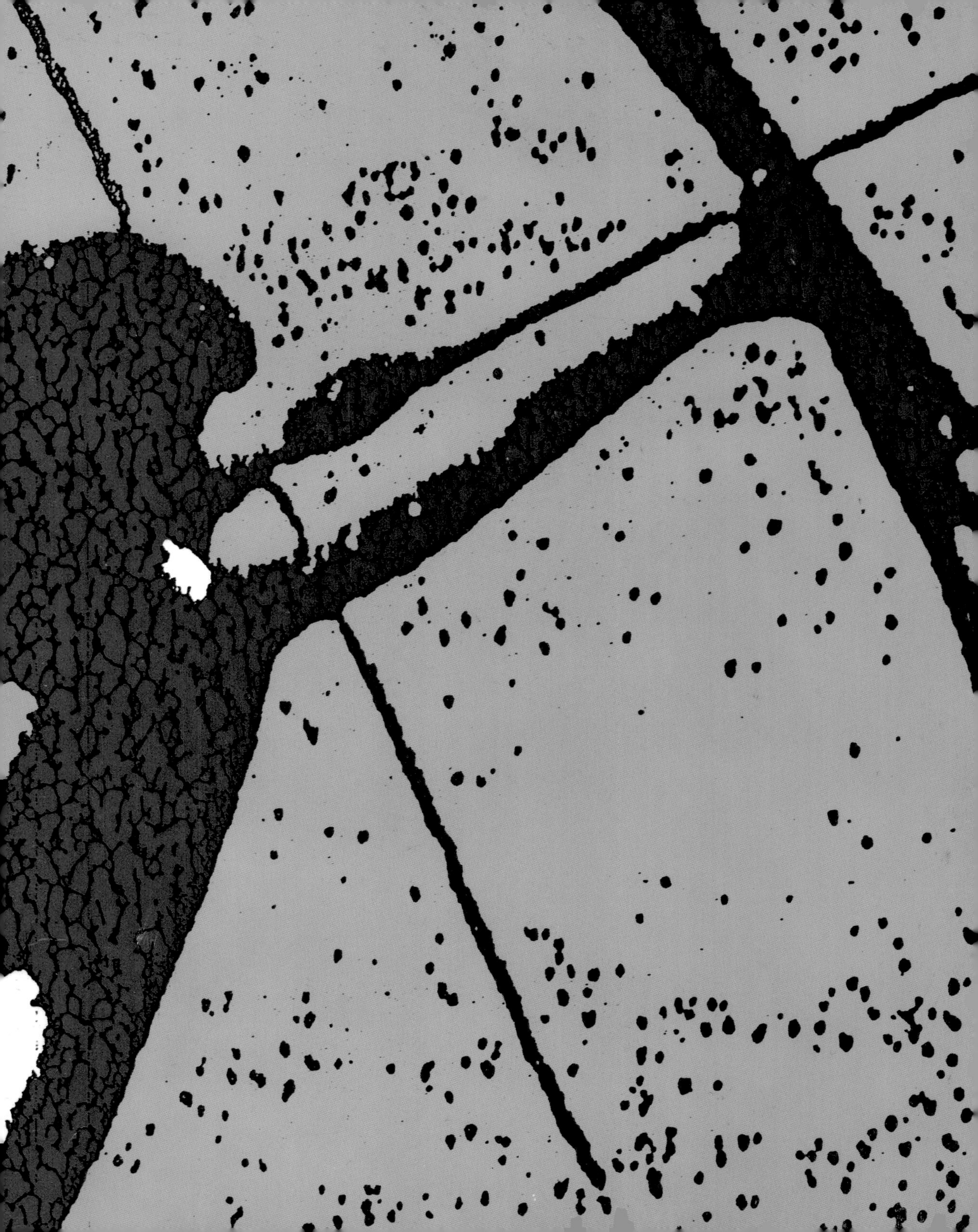

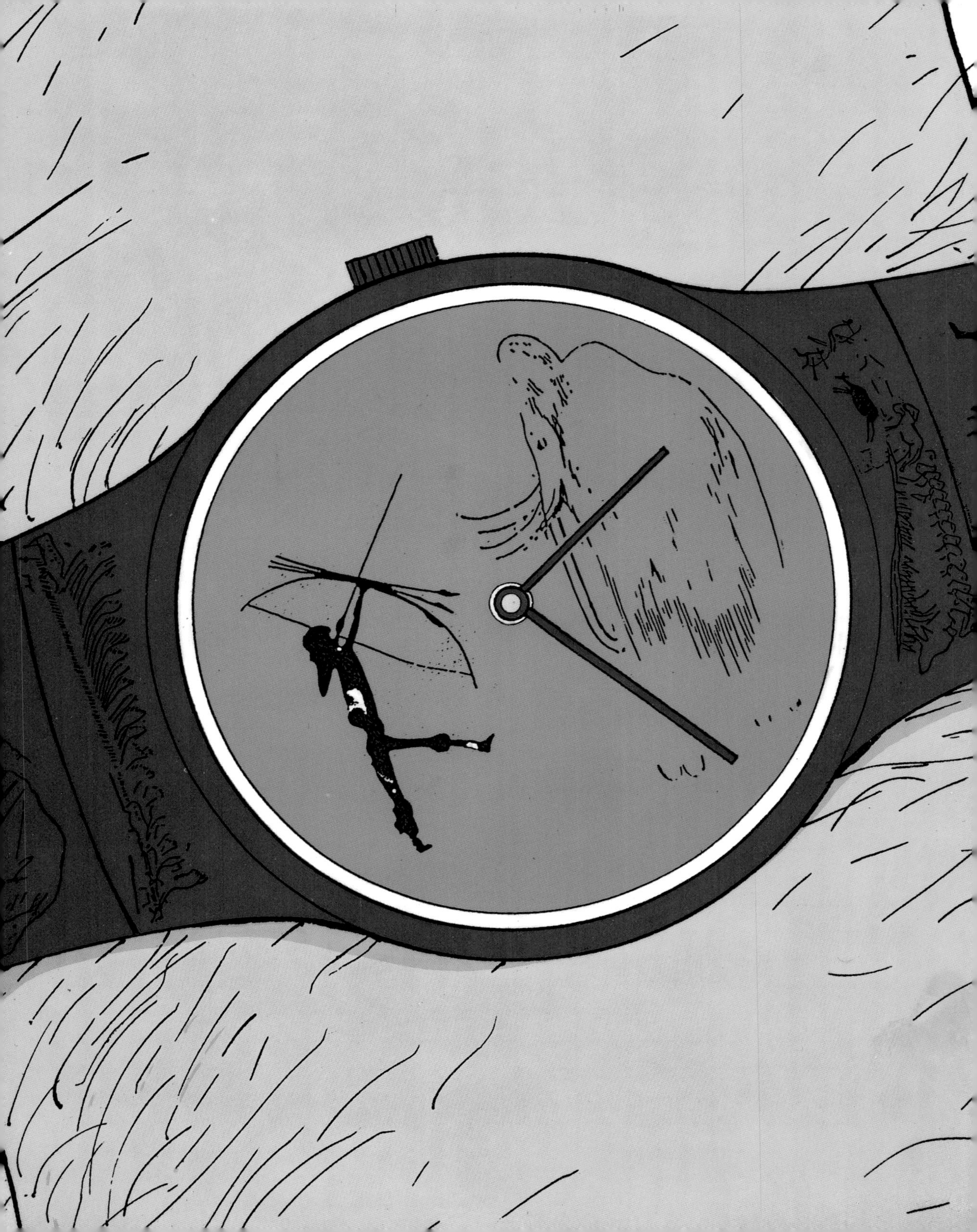

FELIX

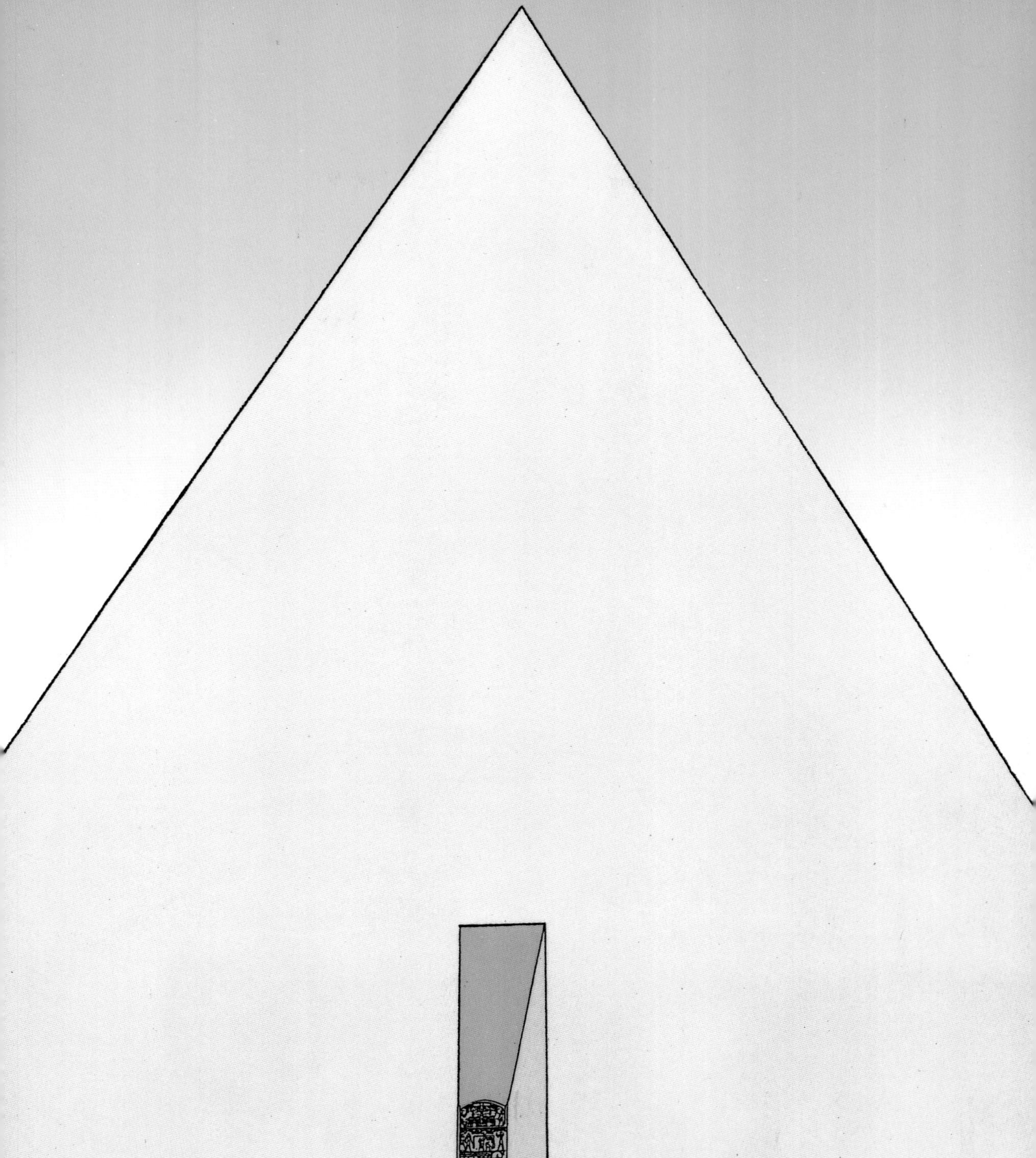

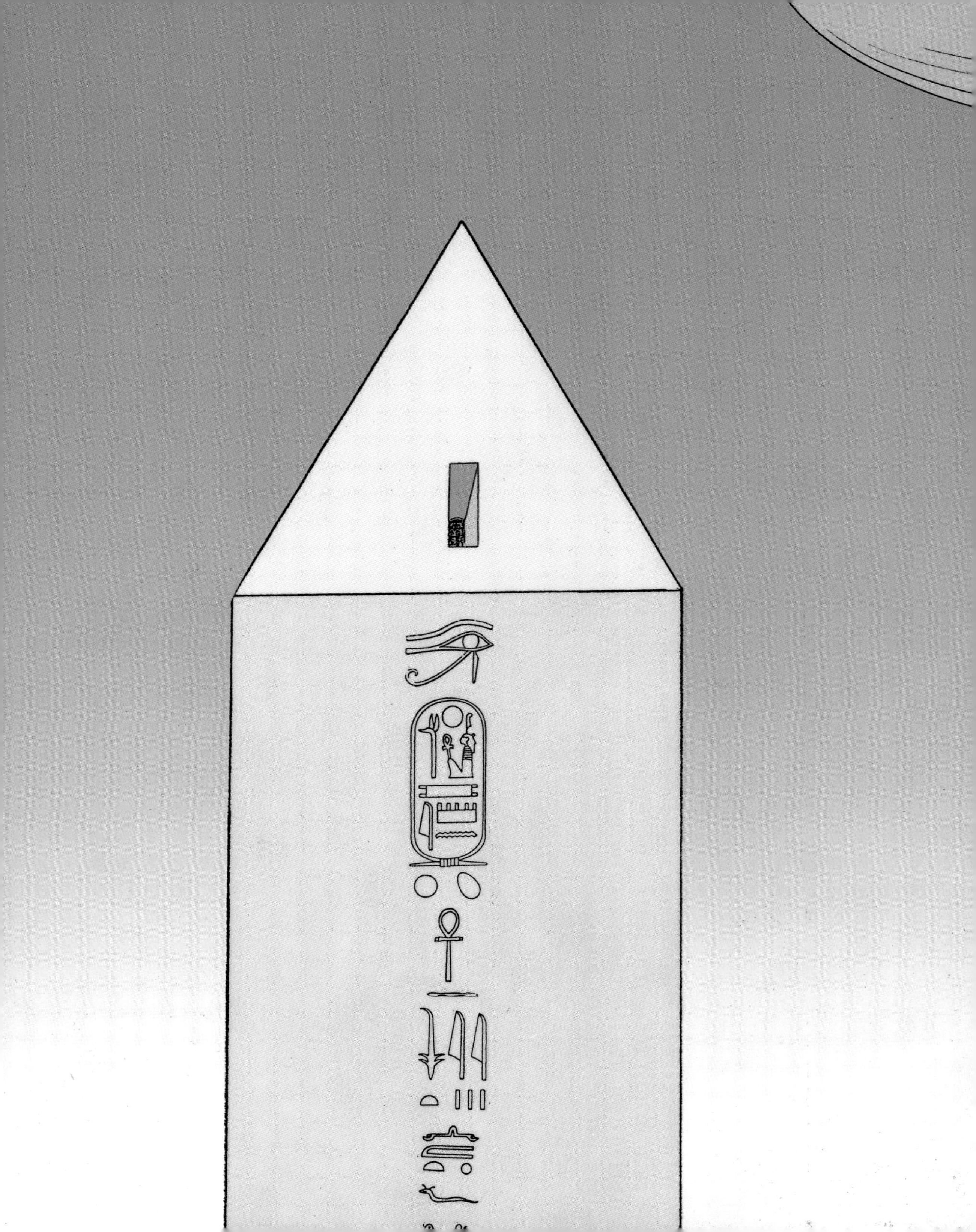

GOODYEAR

PLACE DE LA CONCORDE 1789
EGALITE
18 36

PARIS

PARIS

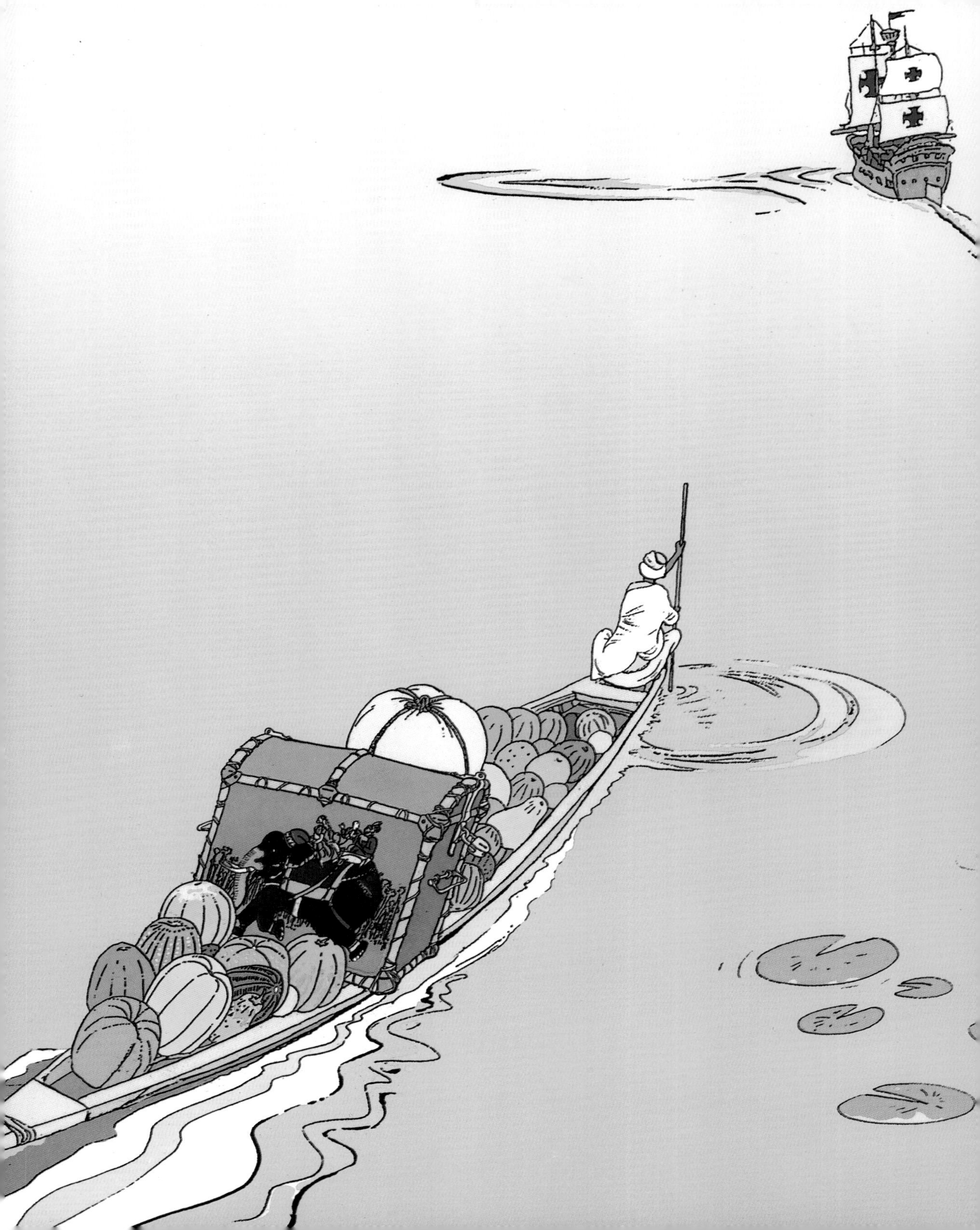

NEW ORLEAN

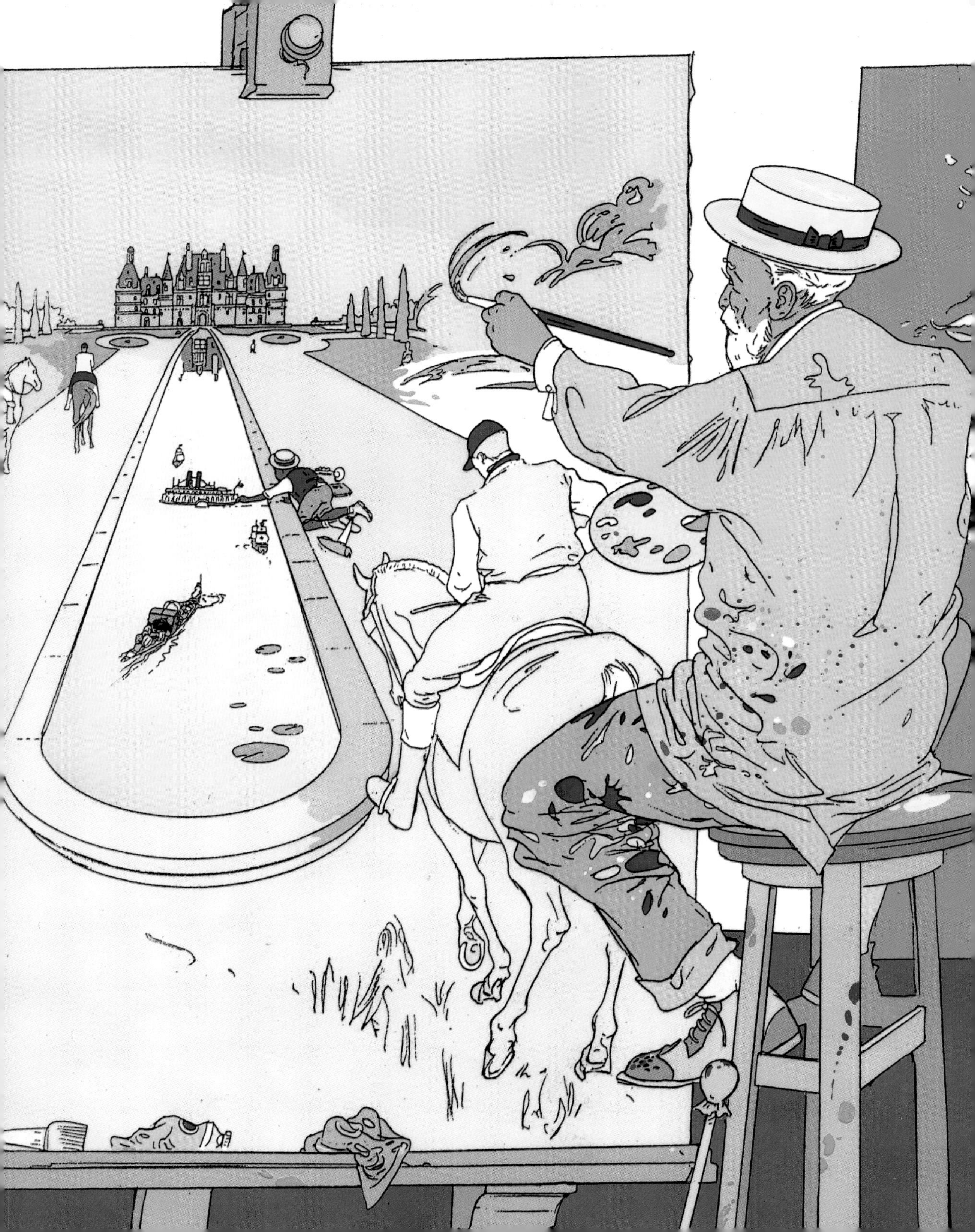

1(800) RE-ZOOM

1(800) RE-ZOOM

RE-ZOOM

2

FREE JAZZ
NEW